ORCAS MAGICAL UNDERWATER WORLD COLORING BOOK

THIS BOOK BELONGS TO:

....

....

....

TEST THE COLORS

www.ingramcontent.com/pod-product-compliance
Lightning Source LLC
Chambersburg PA
CBHW081129080526
44587CB00021B/3810
9781739033811